Look Back at Old Bedwas *and* Trethomas

by
Derrick Jones, Tony Jukes and Gordon Maslen

Volume 1

Foreword by
Wayne David
M.P. for Caerphilly

Old Bakehouse Publications

Abertillery

First published in November 2007

ISBN 978-1-905967-05-6

Published in the U.K. by
Old Bakehouse Publications
Church Street,
Abertillery, Gwent NP13 1EA
Telephone: 01495 212600 Fax: 01495 216222
Email: theoldbakeprint@btconnect.com
Website: www.oldbakehouseprint.co.uk

Made and printed in the UK
by J.R. Davies (Printers) Ltd.

Foreword

by Wayne David M.P.

HOUSE OF COMMONS

Bedwas and Trethomas, separately, have a wealth of history; together they have an abundance. And, there is no better way of making that history real than through old photographs.

Such photographs are frozen glimpses of the past which give an insight into so many facets of how things were. A photograph shows us not only buildings and people who are usually long gone, they also convey, more clearly than words can ever do, the character, the style, emotion, preoccupations and values of by-gone ages.

This collection, painstakingly gathered over many years by enthusiasts who love the communities of which they are part, traces the history of Bedwas and Trethomas from their earliest days to relatively recent times. Taken as a whole they show how these villages have changed, usually, but not always some would say, for the better. They demonstrate that our forebears, through struggle and hard work, created communities out of individuals who were flung together when agriculture was supplanted by the coal industry, and then when a more diverse economy created a more diffuse society.

This book deserves to be widely read, enjoyed and cherished for the gem which it is.

Wayne David
MP for Caerphilly

September 2007

Contents

FOREWORD

INTRODUCTION

Introduction

Until the 1840s the only coal mines in Bedwas were in the upper coal measures in the north of the parish, and then this coal was found in the Caerphilly basin. In little more than 70 years Bedwas changed from a parish largely dependent on agriculture to a vibrant community whose existence depended on coal. There was also the creation of a new settlement to be called Trethomas. A bitter fight began in the late 1920s between the South Wales Miners' Federation and the owners of the colliery and the 'company's union', the South Wales Miners' Industrial Union, to establish the right of the Federation to represent the Bedwas men. Many local men ceased to be employed at Bedwas Colliery and left for employment in the new industrial estates and car manufacturing plants of Oxford, Slough and Dagenham, and the new steel town of Corby before the dispute was finally settled in the late 1930s. With the closure of collieries by the NCB in the 1950s and 1960s many miners were offered employment at Bedwas and new houses were built for them along Lanfabon Drive. Bedwas colliery was closed after the miners' strike of 1984-85 and the communities are now dependent on light industry and the service industry.

The Bedwas and Trethomas Local History Group was formed at a meeting in the Methodist Church in Bedwas in December 1997 to record these changes. It was decided to link the two communities of Bedwas and Trethomas by holding alternate monthly meetings in the Bedwas Methodist Church and the Bryn Pensioners' Hall in Trethomas. Tony Jukes was appointed chairman, Gordon Maslen as secretary, and Derrick Jones became a member of our fledgling committee. Our lecture topics cover a variety of subjects in South-East Wales.

Gordon Maslen's ancestry is typical of many families that moved to Bedwas and Trethomas over the years. His father's family were the Rooms who came from Somerset to work in Bryngwyn Colliery and the Maslens, stonemasons, who came from Wiltshire via Bristol to build the local infrastructure and worked in both the quarries and the pits. His mother's family were the Williams' from Blaenavon who moved down from north Monmouthshire, as did many other families, some bringing strong trade union beliefs. Derrick Jones' father was a cinema projectionist in a workmen's hall in the Rhondda Valley who came to Trethomas in 1942 to be the projectionist in the Workmen's Hall cinema. Derrick's long interest in photography and his copying of old photographs over many years made him an ideal choice as our photograph archivist. Tony Jukes came to the area in 1970 as a research chemist at the Waterloo Works of Coates Brothers and Company Ltd., another vanished industry. As a keen historian he immersed himself in local history, leading an excavation of the Rudry iron furnace by the Oxford House (Risca) Industrial Archaeology Society and attended local history classes taught by the late Don Harris at Bedwas Community College in the early 1970s. A decade later he was teaching those same classes.

The compilation of a photographic album such as this, which comprises many different photographs and subjects, leaves us indebted to the very many people who, for thirty years or more, have allowed us to copy their treasured family pictures and thereby provided valuable information. It could not be done without them. We trust that we have correctly identified all the people in the photographs. Over the years we have been asked many times when were we going to publish such a book. At long last, here it is! We hope you enjoy it. Any profit from the sale of this book will go to the Bedwas and Trethomas Local History Group.

CHAPTER 1

The Village and Farms

1. An Aerial Photograph of Trethomas in 1971.
The coke works is being enlarged by the construction of a battery of 13 ovens on the east end of the original battery of 35 ovens at a cost of £500,000. NCB Housing has now been built and the Colliery Washery has been commissioned. The Pensioners Chalet is visible. The prefabs off Standard Street are still standing, now the site of The Grove sheltered housing complex.

2. The parish poorhouse in the late 1890s.
Before the formation of the Newport Union and the building of the workhouse in Newport, the care of the poor was the responsibility of the parish. This building stood at the entrance to St Barrwg's Church and was listed on the 1841 Bedwas tithe map as inhabited by the poor of the parish. It was later converted into two houses, with a shop licensed to sell tobacco and cigarettes. Note the flat cap and clogs.

3. Bedwas Bridge in 1904.
A timber bridge across the Rhymney River was replaced by this stone bridge built by David Edwards in 1794, son of William Edwards who built the famous bridge at Pontypridd. It cost £80, shared between Bedwas parish and the hamlet of Van. The occasion was probably a baptism in the river before coal washeries polluted the water.

4. Bedwas Square, about 1930.
On the right hand side are Bridge House, the lane leading to the Glebe Farm or Church Farm, and a pair of houses built in 1866 and extended at the front in 1913 to create shops. They were demolished to build the by-pass. Beyond the shops is the Crown Stores, built in 1865 by Mesheck Davies who ran horse omnibuses to Newport, and now a dental practice. A cyclist stands in front of the village water pump just inside the lane.

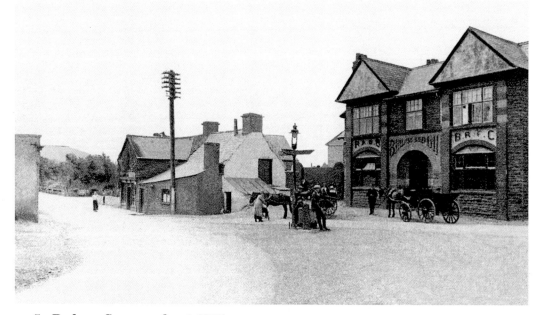

5. Bedwas Square, about 1915.
The driver of the horse brake would wait in the Bridge End Inn until he had collected sufficient passengers. The boys are sitting on the horse watering trough, beneath the finger post. Telephones have arrived. As yet, there are no pavements and only gravel roads, which seemed always to be either very dusty or very muddy.

6. Corker's Cottage, Bedwas Square.
The 'Corker' was the School Truant Officer. This cottage was situated behind the Bridge End Inn at what is now the entrance to the public car park. Note the stone tile roof and lime washed garden walls.

7. Newport Road, Bedwas, late 1930s.
Will Rogers, garage proprietor and plumber, stands at his gate chatting to a member of the Room family. The Newport Cooperative Industrial Society has moved from Church Street to these much larger premises, where it remained in business until the 1970s. The horse-drawn van with pneumatic tyres outside the Bridge End Inn is probably Coleman's bread van from Caerphilly and what appears to be an Austin 7 van which belonged to Jones' Bakery of Caerphilly.

8. Church Street, about 1915.

Note the telephone could be used at the Post Office. A horse and trap waits outside the Bridge End Inn. Bedwas Junior School, opened in 1903, has a cupola which was later removed. A bill board advertises the 'Queen's Courtiers' at the Palace Cinema. In the middle distance, a laburnum tree can be seen which gave the name to 'Golden Chain Cottages' (No.s 35-37). The Wesleyan Chapel was completed in 1897. The shop on the right was built in 1865 by William Thomas, tailor, and at this time kept by his widow Frances. It became Barclays Bank in 1921.

9. The original Bridge End Inn.
The inn was demolished in 1901 to build the present public house. In the picture (left to right) are: ? Joplin, Tal Cosslett (of Rose Cottage), ? Cook, 'Dr' Davies the herbalist, Phoebe Davies (later Mrs Morgan), an unidentified child, William Davies the innkeeper, and Jack Thomas (Phoebe's brother, who kept the 'Red Cow' in Caerphilly) on the pony and trap. Corker's Cottage is just visible on the right hand side of the inn.

10. Church Street, in 1913.
Bound's grocery shop is on the right at the corner with East Avenue. They also sold fish and chips. In the 1930s, the shop became Pavlov's Hay, Corn and Flour Merchants. On the left are Golden Chain Cottages with their laburnum tree, No. 3 being later converted into a haberdashery, run by Miss Jervis, Victoria House, a double-fronted shop currently the Post Office, and the Wesleyan Methodist church completed in 1897. Further up can be seen Lewis's Butchers Shop, named Oakfield House and Bethel Chapel, opened in 1903. The newly formed Bedwas and Machen UDC widened Church Street to provide footpaths in 1913 and the drains are being laid with salt-glazed pipes.

11. Bedwas from Brewery Terrace, 1907.
The Police Station (1910) has yet to be built. Bakers Row is visible on the left. In the centre is the 'Top Shop' with its storehouse and bakehouse. On the right is the Oak Field, one of the village's first sports fields, with the oak tree that gave its name. Lewis the Butchers had their shop in Oakfield House with an abattoir behind it. The detached cottages on Pandy Road, (distant right) are amongst the oldest in Bedwas. Newport Road and Pandy Road are beginning to grow. The stables at the beginning of East Avenue (now the Surgery) were used for stabling the Council's horse and cart and served as a 'band room'.

12. Tydfil Road, about 1910.
The yard of Williams Brothers, builders, is on the right. The shop on the right was owned by Edmunds, haberdashers, and the striped pole advertises the presence of barber Tom Davies. Further up the road, women are taking in a delivery of coal. A horse and cart is making another coal delivery further along. Building is still on-going on the left. The road was named after Elen Tydfil Davies, the only daughter of Dr Joseph Davies of Ty Isaf.

13. Trethomas from Rudry, mid-1950s.
Gwaun-y-Bara Farm is in the foreground. The grid lay-out of Trethomas, its roads named after Sir Williams James Thomas and his wife, can be clearly seen, together with post-war 'prefabs'. Just below the British Benzol Plant are the houses of colliery officials, Ty'n-y-wern Terraces, often called 'White City' (tongue in cheek!). The distillation plant and gasometers lie to the left of the ovens.
On the far left are the colliery cooling towers, demolished when the winding operations were electrified in the early 1960s.

14. Hillside Terrace and Bedwas, about 1920.
The first private houses at the beginning of Hillside Terrace were built by Williams Brothers in 1909. The council houses are not built. On Bryn Gwyn Street can just be seen a building with a circular window which was the original stables for the horses change on the Rhymney Tramroad, for Rosser Thomas's Carn Gethin colliery (Tir-y-Berth). The stables, with double doors wide enough for a cart, were later used for rehearsals by the Bedwas Silver Band.

15. Construction of the new council houses on Hillside Terrace in the 1920s.
Bedwas and Machen Urban District Council Bedwas acquired part of the glebe land by compulsory purchase in 1922 and began to build new housing for the growing population of the area.

16. The new council houses, in the 1930s.
This view of East Avenue and The Crescent was taken from the tump that was originally behind the Pentecostal Church. The track in the foreground ran from Glebe Street to the Workmen's Hall.

17. Prefabs on Standard Street, Trethomas.
The housing shortage after the Second World War caused many local authorities to opt for prefabricated bungalows or 'prefabs'. They were relatively cheap, quick to construct and very comfortable. Trethomas and Bedwas had several streets of them. Many people regretted their demise.

18. Construction of William Street, Trethomas.
On the left is Mr. Richards who collected the rent. On the right is George West, Rose
Kibby's father, building foreman, who lived in the first house.

19. Newport Road, Trethomas, in 1982.
The heavy snowfall of 1982 brought almost everything to a halt. A queue for bread
quickly formed at the 'Oven Door', later Glanmor's, for freshly baked bread.

20. Persondy, Rectory Road.
'Persondy' is Welsh for Parson's House. This was the first rectory in Bedwas. For many years the Bishop of Llandaff appointed himself rector, taking the considerable rents of the glebe land and paying a curate to officiate in the parish, hence Persondy. The tithe barn once stood to the left, where once farmers brought a tenth of their produce for the benefit of clergy and parish. The thatch roof was burned off in December 1857 by a spark from a steam engine. Stone from the ruins was used to construct the church car park and memorial garden at the entrance to St Barrwg's after the demolition of the poorhouse.

21. Rectory Road, about 1910.
The Rectory is just hidden by a row of pine trees. Rector William Williams borrowed £850 from Queen Anne's Bounty, which was set up to provide suitable houses for the use of benefices, and also mortgaged the glebe rents and tithes to build a new Rectory and other necessary offices in 1857 upon the glebe land belonging to the church.

22. Newport Road, Trethomas in the 1950s.
The shops before yellow lines and parking restrictions.

23. Central Buildings, Newport Road, Trethomas.
These buildings were completed in 1914. Wolfson's Gents Outfitters supplied the Trethomas Bluebirds with playing kit over several seasons. Next to it was the India and China Tea shop. Next to E.C. Davies (Meurig Stores) was Starr's grocery shop, later taken over by Peter Bulgin. Note the original position of the public telephone kiosk, a Standard Ensign car and bikes on the kerb.

24./25. Two cottages in Bedwas which were demolished in 1935.
Mr W.B. Hirst wrote to the *South Wales Argus*, enclosing photographs, to protest that these cottages had been allowed to fall into the hands of the 'house-breaking gangs'. The upper picture is of Pen Cae'r Eglwys, which stood just below Bryn Heulog (visible behind), and the lower one is of Pen Heol Bedwas at the corner of Mountain Road and Cwm Road, one of the last thatched houses in Bedwas.

26. Ty'n-y-wern Farm and the Coking Plant.
Ty'n-y-Wern farm was part of the Tredegar Estate, and last occupied by the Davies
family. Here it is surrounded by the construction of the benzol plant, alongside the
coking works, in the late 1920s. It gave its name to the Junior School that was built on
its land. The colliery company used the farm buildings for a period before they were
finally demolished.

27. Trehir thatched cottage, 1935.
Thatch had been used in the village but was rapidly disappearing by the 1920s. This was Trehir Cottage in 1935, near Trehir Farm, Pandy Lane, one of the last remaining examples. It has since been replaced by a bungalow.

28. The Glebe Farm or Church Farm.
From left to right are the beast house, the hay barn, the Glebe farmhouse, sometimes referred to as Church Farm since glebe land was originally owned by the church, and Bridgefield House.

29. Ty Maen Farm.
Ty Maen was part of the Tredegar Estate and could be reached via Penywaun Farm or via Cats Lane. This view of the farm is from Cats Lane.

30. Haymaking at Ty Maen farm, about 1922.
Left to right: Charles Nash, Bill Harding, ?, Mrs Deborah Nash, Tom Williams ('Tommy Ty Maen'), Mrs Lawrence (wife of the colliery engineer), Emlyn Meyrick, Ceinwen Davies (nee Williams), ?, Arthur Martin (behind), Billy Nash. Emlyn Meyrick lived at Plas Potta Cottage before moving to Berllanllwyd.

31. Bedwas Fawr, about 1915.
George Rowlands the farmer is at the gate. The other man is possibly Mr Potter the
rating officer for Bedwas and Machen UDC.

32. Bedwas Fawr, in 1969.
This was one of the oldest farms in the area, dating back to the Tudor period. It was
demolished in 1971 to make way for the Bedwas House Industrial Estate. The farm
originally had a malt house for malting barley prior to brewing.

(Photograph courtesy of Glyndwr G Jones)

33. A smallholding alongside the Colliery Road, in the late 1930s.
The smallholding with its hayrick was farmed by Dick Edmunds of Felin Fach Farm.
Businesses required grazing for the carriage horses and Dick Edmunds later went into
lorry transport. The corrugated hut of the South Wales Miners' Federation (the 'Fed
Hut') erected outside the colliery's boundary during the long dispute with the colliery
company, can be seen next to Sebastopol Cottages.

34. Dr Joseph Davies of Ty Isaf.
Dr Joseph Davies (1793-1873), of Ty Isaf is depicted with his fox hounds on Mynydd
Hafod-Tudor near Mynyddislwyn Church in an oil painting, probably by Mulloch of
Newport of about 1855. Because of his lifestyle, Monmouthshire newspapers often
referred to him as 'Baron Bedwas'.

35. Haymaking at Glyngwyn Farm in 1906.
Glyn Gwyn farm was owned by Sir James Thomas and supplied hay for the ponies at his Ynyshir Colliery in the Rhondda Valley. This photo was taken in 1906. Many of the workers were probably sent down from Ynyshir to help with haymaking.
(Photo courtesy of the Stephen Rowson Collection)

36. Harvesting in the fields along Mountain Road during the Second World War.
The Edmunds girls, Maggie and Gladys of Felin Fach Farm, help with haymaking, using a tractor from before the modern era of rubber tyres. 'Rockleize' is in the background.

37. Pandy Mawr.

This very old farm was inherited by Ann Alldworth, granddaughter of John Greenuff who leased Machen forge and Caerphilly furnace. By her will dated 1729 she endowed the Alldworth Charity with her lands to establish, a school for the girls of the parishes of Eglwysilan and Bedwas. The school was situated in Pandy Mawr from 1809 to 1884.

38. Pantglas Farm, 1968.

John Wesley preached here in 1749. The door in the porch was barred with a heavy beam of wood fitting into a socket, and the cheese room was above. The John family (Tom John) were the last occupants. The farm was demolished in 1968 to make way for the Pantglas Industrial Estate.

(Photograph courtesy of Glyndwr Jones)

39. A Ploughing Match on Glyn Rhymney Farm in 1981.

The Mynyddislwyn and District Ploughing Match Society held their event at Glyn Rhymney Farm in 1981. John Davies (1795-1866), younger brother of Dr. Joseph Davies of Ty Isaf, married Elizabeth Thomas of Glyn Rhymney in 1819, a widow 25 years his senior, and rebuilt the farm (the barn has a date stone 1823). He was a generous benefactor of Cardiff Royal Infirmary and bequeathed £1000 to endow a school for boys in Bedwas. John Gibbon of the Glebe farm purchased Glyn Rhymney in 1931 and it is now farmed by Howard Gibbon and his family.

40. Ty'n-y-Coed Farm.

A farm near Maesycwmmer when that village was classed as the Bedwas Upper division of Bedwas parish.

CHAPTER 2

Industry

41. Lighting up the first coke ovens at Bedwas, October 1929.
A group of Woodhall-Duckham representatives and Bedwas Navigation Colliery senior officials, including Company Secretary Griffith Morgan (2nd left in rear), plant manager D.M. Hughes (sitting extreme left) and Mrs Hughes (standing extreme right) on the occasion of the commissioning of the first coke ovens.

42. Bryngwyn Colliery pumping engine house.
The Bryngwyn Colliery was one of ten collieries in the Caerphilly basin working a downfold of the Maesycwmmer seam of the Upper Coal measures, known locally as the Llantwit seam and a good house coal. The Cornish pumping engine house was erected by colliery owner W.S. Cartwright in 1868. The engine house, the northwest corner of which collapsed in 1979, is undergoing preservation work by Charles Church Ltd. builders.

43. Bryngwyn Colliery pumping engine house and chimney.
The colliery, near the end of its working life, closed in 1893 after a strike which lasted six months. Closure of many of the surrounding collieries meant that considerable pumping was required at great cost. Rosser Thomas continued to win coal from the pillars above the water line until the colliery finally closed in 1908.

44. Bryngwyn colliery.
The Bryngwyn colliery viewed from above the Barry Railway Company's Llanbradach viaduct, here under construction in 1906. Alongside the Brecon and Merthyr railway and the waste tip are the haulage engine, workshop and offices, with the manager's house, Graig Villa to the right. The haulage engine pulled trams of coal and waste out of the drift alongside the pumping engine house and up the incline to the railway and the waste tip.

45. The Bryngwyn colliery pumping engine house and drift.
As it might have looked in the late nineteenth century, as drawn by Michael Blackmore.
(Photograph courtesy of the late David Bick who commissioned this work)

Tons.   Cwt

No._____

FROM THE
DIAMOND LLANTWIT COLLIERY Co.,
BEDWAS.

Consignee_____

_____

Via_____

Date,_____ 189

46. Diamond Llantwit waybill.
A coal wagon waybill from the Diamond Llantwit Colliery in Trethomas. Thomas Thomas leased the coal under Glyngwyn farm after the failure of the Bedwas and Llantwit Coal Company in 1872 and set up the Diamond Llantwit Colliery Company. This colliery closed after the miners' strike in 1892, although the pillars were worked with a few men until about 1902.

47. Sir William James Thomas (1867-1947).
James Thomas (1817-1901), a farmer's son, began working in the pits at the age of 6 as a door boy. In 1850 he became a partner in a colliery in the Rhondda Valley and made his fortune after opening the Ynyshir colliery in 1877. His grandson William James Thomas gained his experience at Ynyshir and inherited the collieries, assuming full control in 1901. He made generous donations and endowments to many hospitals including the Netley hospital for war injured servicemen and was knighted in 1914. He formed the Bedwas Navigation Colliery Company Ltd in 1910. The streets in Trethomas are named after him.

48. Bedwas colliery in 1911.
The power house has been erected, both shafts are being sunk, and the other surface buildings are under construction. The design and engineering work was by Edmund L. Hann, later to become chairman of the Powell Duffryn Company, and was a copy in design principle of Penallta Colliery. His father Edmund M. Hann was a brilliant engineer and General Manager of Collieries at P.D.

49. Bedwas Colliery in 1912.
Most of the construction work has been completed but the colliery is not yet open as sinking work in the south shaft is still ongoing (evidenced by a single sheaf) and the sidings are clean. Fred Piggott was in charge of sinking the pits and his house later became the Caerphilly Miners' Hospital.

50. Bedwas colliery, 1936.
Trams of coal were emptied by tipplers in the covered area around the south pit onto the picking belt, where stone, timber and other waste was removed, and then tipped into railway wagons. The ramp took pit wood from the timber yard to the shafts to be taken underground.

51. The 1912 accident.
The scene at the pithead after the first serious accident at Bedwas colliery on Wednesday, March 27th 1912. An explosion of gas and fire seriously burnt 12 men, several of whom later died.

52. Thomastown pit, about 1914.
Trethomas was known as Thomastown for a short period but the name was changed to avoid confusion with Thomastown in the Rhondda Valley. Below the cooling tower is the Dark Arch under the Brecon and Merthyr railway and colliery sidings which gave access to the pit from Trethomas.

53. Bedwas pit bank group, 1924.
Back row (left to right): Thomas John Williams, Idris Thomas (winder), ?, Garnet Ridout (powerhouse foreman), Fred Watts, Charlie England, Charlie Morris (power-house cleaner). Front row (left to right): ?, John Dineen (winder), John Brimscombe (banksman), Harry Haines (fan man).

54. Sir Samuel Instone (1878-1937).
His first business venture had been a London shipping company and then coal sales from Newport and Cardiff. The Bedwas Navigation Colliery Company Ltd. was in financial difficulties because of a downturn in the coal trade after World War One and geological problems. In 1921 the colliery was purchased by S. Instone and Company Ltd. and Instone became chairman of the reformed Bedwas Navigation Colliery Company (1921) Ltd. Initially he was a benevolent employer and a generous patron of the Workmen's Hall. As the price of coal fell during the 1920s the Company became more determined to increase profitability. Barclays Bank had loaned the company £1M and in 1928 the bank's representative H. Stuart Martin was appointed a director. The owners refused to recognize the South Wales Miners' Federation, and thus began a period of unrest and confrontation in Bedwas which was to last over a decade. *(Courtesy of the National Portrait Gallery, London).*

55. Powerhouse group, 1915.
Back row (L to R): Harry Haines, ?, Joe Davies, ?, Wyndham Cottrell. Front row: Louis Rees, John Denine, Cecil Ellis, ? Morris.

56. The Powerhouse viewed from the overhead gantry, February 1937.
In front on the left is a Brown-Bovery stand-by generator with a rotary converter visible on the edge of the picture, a Roby air compressor, an old steam-driven compressor with flywheel which was not used much as it was only low pressure, and the north pit winder. On the right are the main power generator, a small generator and stand-by generator, the main switchboard, and an Alley McClachan compressor which was used in conjunction with the Roby when the Parsons compressor was in trouble.

57. Parsons Turbine Compressor, 1934.
In front (left to right) are Reg Ellis (switchboard attendant), Joe Davis (winder, north pit), Trevor Thomas, Cliff Richards (cleaner, later winding engine man), Gwynfor Jones, Stan Salisbury (powerhouse foreman), and Jack West (assistant general foreman). Behind the Parsons compressor, average speed 3300-3400 rpm, is an Alley triple expansion compressor which worked at 115-120 rpm.

58. A blacksmith at Bedwas Colliery.
Edward Thomas George was one of the first blacksmiths to be employed at Bedwas Colliery. He was born in Cwmdows, near Newbridge, and went to live at Porset when he was 5 years old. His father was employed as a blacksmith at the old Rhos Llantwit Colliery at Porset, where he learnt his trade. He was a registered shoeing smith, winning many prizes in competitions, and a member of the Caerphilly Town Silver Band. He worked until the age of 70 and is seen here making a drag hook for the colliery trams.

59. A group of colliers and workmen.
Photographed in the bracken at the back of the colliery in the 1920s.

60. Federation Hut and Dark Arch.
The South Wales Miners' Federation had a hut just outside the Dark Arch during the long dispute with Instone and the Miners Industrial Union, where colliers were asked to show their SWMF cards.

61./62. Mounted police escorting 'blackleg' workmen home on Newport Road.

The 1920s was a difficult time for the coal industry and frequent disputes between the owners and a militant Bedwas lodge of the Federation brought lock-outs in 1930 and 1932. Contractors and 'strangers' began to be employed. In February 1933 the company entered into an agreement with the Miners' Industrial Union, and a condition of employment was membership of the MIU and union dues subtracted from wages. The police had to escort the increasing numbers of 'blacklegs' home through crowds hurling abuse and giving them a 'panning'. On Friday 17th March 1933 stones were thrown at 'blacklegs' and their police escorts, and extra police reinforcements were brought in. The following day a brick hit one of the 'blacklegs' and police went into the crowd, arresting two women and taking them to Bedwas Police Station. A large angry crowd assembled in Church Street which the police dispersed by a baton charge after magistrate Edgar Lewis read the Riot Act.

63. Mounted police escorting 'blackleg' workmen home along Navigation Street.

64. Police at Bedwas in 1935.
This group of policemen was photographed behind the colliery as the troubles continued. They used army-type wooden huts behind the lamp room for rest and sleep during their period of duty. When the South Wales Miners' Federation called a strike in the coalfield in September 1936 to force Sir Samuel Instone to hold a ballot to ask the miners which union they wanted to represent them, over 200 members of the Industrial Union signed up to use the huts rather than risk leaving the colliery.

65. Mounted police at Bedwas.
A group of mounted policemen at Bedwas during the colliery dispute in 1933. The men and horses were quartered at Glyn Gwyn farm, which was the colliery farm.

66. Men leaving the pit on the Colliery road, September 1936.
The Federation had given notice that all its members were being called out on strike on Monday September 7th throughout the coalfield, although it was expected that members of the Industrial Union would continue working at Bedwas and Taff Merthyr collieries. Federation members at Bedwas staged a stay-down strike on Thursday, September 3rd, a tactic first used in the South Wales coalfield at Nine Mile Point colliery in 1935, to cripple the colliery. The strike ended on the Saturday evening after 60 hours underground. Men are pictured here leaving via the Colliery road, the gate guarded by a police officer.

67./68. The end of the stay-down strike at Bedwas Colliery, 1936.
After many meetings with all parties concerned in the dispute, the Secretary for Mines brokered a deal whereby Sir Samuel Instone would meet with the Federation under a neutral chairman to discuss holding a ballot of miners. It was agreed that the strikers would not be victimised or sacked and Federation officials went down the pit to give them the news. 43 men ascended the Rock Vein pit to be greeted by their families and, after collecting their pay at the office, were taken by bus to the Workmen's Hall for a meal and then home. On the left in the top picture is Dewi 'Monkey' Richards.

69. Meeting outside the Workmen's Hall.
Colliers rejoice outside the Bedwas Workmen's Hall after the success of the stay-down strike in September 1936. During the long dispute Sir Samuel Instone tried to prevent their use of the hall.

70. Blacksmiths and men from the engineering shop at Bedwas colliery, 1930s.

71. Coal delivery lorry, 1931.
Dick Edmunds of Felin Fach had the contract to deliver the miners' concessionary house coal. One of his two lorries is seen here with (L to R) Bill Davies, Clem Edmunds and Tom Miles.

72. Colliery rescue team outside the lamp room, 1930s.
Back row (left to right); Colliery Sergeant Edwards, Mr Kitt (in charge), Griffith Morgan, ? Murphy (overman), Joe Matthews (overman), Dai Evans (fireman), John Hill (under manager), ?, Bryn Williams (overman), ?, ? Hale (mechanical engineer), Mr Stacey (manager), ? Jenkins (electrical engineer), Mr Ashurst (agent), Front row (left to right): Latimer Rees (under manager), ? Griffith.

73. Removing the old winder.
In the late 1950s the NCB approved a major reorganisation at the colliery, with new electric winders. The old steam winders and bicylindrical conical (BCC) drums were replaced in 1962, although this photograph appears to show an earlier removal of the North Pit drum judging by the dress and the absence of hard hats.

74. Miners at Bedwas Colliery.
Colliers in the M9 district at Bedwas finishing work at the South Pit in 1960. They are, from left to right, Arthur Rogers, Idwal Harding, Don Pole and Des Olsen.

75. Colliery Queen.
The NCB's Colliery Queen at Bedwas pit bottom in January 1972. Second from the
right is Stan Blackwell.

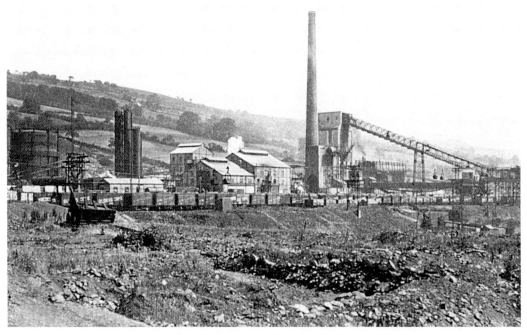

76. The benzol distillation and coke works at Trethomas in the late 1930s.
Sir Samuel Instone formed British Benzol and Coal Distillation Ltd in 1928 and
erected this plant to produce coke and by-products from Bedwas coal in 1929. As a
separate company it escaped nationalisation in 1947 and ceased production on
Christmas Eve 1985.

77. Bedwas coke works, 1928.
The chimney and bunker are under construction. One man was killed when he fell from the chimney.

78. The benzol distillation plant.
The works made foundry coke, much of which was sold in the Midlands. The gaseous effluent from the top of the coke ovens was scrubbed to remove ammonia, which was neutralised with sulphuric acid to make fertiliser. The coal gas or 'town gas' was used at the pit but later pumped to Newport and then to the Caerphilly tar plant. The benzol distillation plant refined the crude benzol. Crude tar was distilled at Caerphilly.

79. Timber salvage yard, 1945.
This photo shows a group of Bedwas and Trethomas men and women working in the open by the Workmen's Hall breaking up old packing cases brought from Newport to recover the timber. They are (L to R): Alice Price, Stan Roden, Nick White, Olive Gadd, Beat Evans, Mrs. Gains, Graham Rees, Phyllis Jones, Linda Chisholm, Ann Harris, Mrs. Cornish, and Mrs. Gilbert.

80. MeGlaPlas workers.
MeGlaPlas Ltd came to Bedwas in 1947 and brought new employment, taking over the old cinema and adjoining buildings for the manufacture of small metal pressings and stampings for cigarette cases and lighters, later making specialist pressings for domestic appliances, toys and office system accessories.

CHAPTER 3

Transport

81. Grocer's Delivery Bicycle. The delivery bike was an invaluable way of quickly delivering orders around the village without the need of a horse and cart. W. D. Cosslett's shop was in Victoria House, now the Post Office in Church Street.

82. The Caerphilly horse brake, about 1914.
A regular horse and carriage service operated to Caerphilly in the late nineteenth century/early twentieth century. The horses were probably stabled at the Bridge End Inn. The driver, Alf Miles, waited in the bar until the carriage was full. Standing in front of the horse is landlord G. Alden. Seated in the brake are Brinmore Jones, Caradoc Jones, Will Masters and J. Morgan. Alf Jones is standing by the rear step and ? Masters and J. Lawrence in the pub doorway.

83. George Rowlands.
George Rowlands farmed Bedwas Fawr. The horse's name was Tommy.

84. The New Bridge.
The old main road from Newport to Caerphilly over Bedwas Bridge eventually proved inadequate and a new road was constructed from Bedwas Square passing over the Rhymney River at the 'New Bridge', a joint undertaking by Monmouthshire and Glamorgan County Highway Authorities. A plaque, now lost, on the bridge commemorated the opening date and marked the county boundaries.

85. Porset toll house.
This Tollgate Cottage stood on the turnpike road from Newport to Caerphilly near Porset Brook. The last resident, Mrs. Thomas, is seen here in Vic Hardacre's photograph. The house was demolished in about 1969.

86. The 'Pike', 1949.
A toll gate was erected on the turnpike next to the Ty'n-y Pwll Inn, now known to all in Trethomas as 'The Pike'. The first signs of the motor car age can be seen in Durston's Garage, with Police Sergeant Fox keeping a watchful eye on developments.

87. Bedwas Square, 1915.
By 1915 the age of the charabanc had arrived and the pleasant prospect of an 'outing', this one setting off from outside the Bridge End Inn. Perhaps the weather was not too good as the covers are 'on'. Note that the pub then sold Pritchard's beers.

88. Starr's Charabanc.
Starr's charabanc of Trethomas was a dual purpose vehicle, used as a lorry for grocery deliveries, then fitted with seats for an 'outing'. The driver in this photograph was Don Meredith, later chauffer to Griffith Morgan, Company Secretary of the Bedwas Navigation Colliery. Dai 'Aberdare' Jones, wearing a trilby, is sat near the front.

89. Bedwas Conservative Club outing, 1934.
Improvements in coach design included the fitting of a roll-top, giving the luxury of ventilation and rain proofing. Alf Miles is on the left.

90. Trethomas coach trip, 1950s.
Even greater luxury came in the 1950s with coaches fitted with a glass roof.

91. A B&M UDC double-decker.

Bedwas and Machen UDC began operating buses in 1922, the smallest fleet operator in the United Kingdom, and yet managed to make a profit! The livery was peacock blue and cream. GWO 482 shown here at the Council Office's garage was an Albion Venturer low bridge 57-seater double-decker with bodywork built by Welsh Metal Industries of Caerphilly in 1948.

92. Drivers and conductresses taking a well earned break.
Left to right: Mauvie Pugh, David 'Dai' Davies, Ron Richards, and Delga Richards.

93. An up train at Bedwas station.
The original Bryn Gwyn houses can be seen in the background. The train carried pupils to Maesycwmmer Secondary School, later to Bedwellty Grammar School and students to New Tredegar Technical College. Many miners came to work at Bedwas Colliery on this line.

94. Bedwas station staff.
This picture shows the signal box, with its decorative finials, the station house and the adjoining Church House Inn. George Sheen is second from the left.

95. Bedwas Railway Station, about 1920.
A view towards Newport at Bedwas Station, with passengers and gas-lighting on the left, and the stationmaster's house, signal box, goods shed and cattle ramp on the right. The siding was used for house coal distribution and was built on the site of the Bedwas Brewery.

96. Trethomas Station, about 1950.
Trethomas Station looking west towards the coke ovens in the near distance. Gas lighting still remains.

97. The east view from Church Street Bridge, 1950s.
On the right beyond the trees are the Old Rectory and Ty Dolwen. In the centre distance are Sebastopol Cottage and the colliery offices. The bridges were the last act of the Rumney tramroad company in its conversion to a railway before purchase by the Brecon and Merthyr Railway Company. They bear the legend Rumney Railway Company 1863 and were built by the Eagle Foundry of Cardiff.

98. Bedwas Colliery signal box.
Looking east toward the colliery and coke ovens. Sebastopol Cottage and the colliery offices are to the left and the colliery sidings to the right. A dramatic incident involved Signalman Fred Watkins, when he suffered a heart attack here whilst on duty. He had the presence of mind to set the signals before collapsing thus preventing a major accident. The signal box was known thereafter as the 'Fred Watkins Box'.

CHAPTER 4

Shops and Shopkeeping

99. Corner shop, Trethomas.
Sited at the corner of Newport Road and Navigation Street, this grocery shop was owned by Joseph Walters in 1912. 'Walters the Milk' also ran a dairy on the opposite side of Newport Road near the Co-operative Building. The Bishop family later acquired the shop for greens and general produce. Later they moved into the wholesale fruit and vegetable business with premises in Glebe Road.

100. 'Top Shop', before 1914.
A general store in Church Street probably purpose built by George Gardiner Lewis in the 1870s with a bakery at the rear. It was a large shop with a wide range of goods, earning it the nickname of 'Top Shop'. A special feature was a wire and tube mechanical transfer system for cash and receipts to a central cashier. On the right of the staff is Floyd Phipps, of Snowdrop Cottage, later killed in World War One.

101. CDS Stores.
This shop at the corner of Church Street and Hillside Terrace was opened in 1912 by Benjamin Rosser, who we believe to be pictured in the doorway. It became the 'CDS' or 'Cash Drapery Stores' run by John Lewis Jones, later a launderette and 'Pets Corner' until recently. The CDS stocked a range of general drapery as well as offering tailoring for made-to-measure men's suits and ladies fashions.

102. Williams Temperance Bar.

Built as a shop on Newport Road, it stood opposite the Pavilion Cinema now occupied by the BTM Band. It was originally opened by Robert 'Bob' Williams, seen here on the right. The Temperance Bar was a by-product of the Temperance Movement in the early decades of the 20th century, offering a range of American soft drinks. The shop did much trade with the cinema audiences where Bob sang to accompany the silent movies, with Horace Rogers as pianist.

103. Sam Phipps, shoemaker.

Sam Phipps at the hut of Harry Pitts the shoemaker, sited near 31 Church Street, where he learned the shoemakers trade. Later he moved to 18 Church Street now occupied by David Buckland, then set up his own hut in East Avenue. Sam was a local preacher at the Wesleyan (Methodist) Chapel. The East Avenue hut was a good place for discussion and help with homework!

104. Mrs. Elizabeth Bevan and Rose Kibby's shop No.3 Newport Road, Trethomas.
Originally owned by Mrs. Collins, it was acquired by the Bevans in 1947 and held till the early 1960s selling newspapers, toys and sweets. This photograph shows Elizabeth 'Betty' Bevan and Rose Kibby. Rose's father was the foreman of the company that built William Street.

105. Lui's Café.
Italians, many of them from the Bardi region of northern Italy, opened cafés throughout South Wales as the coalfield prospered. Lui Rabaiotti's Café in Central Buildings was there from the 1940s. Here Lui is with his wife Eunice. Inside can be seen Henry, Lui's brother. Another brother, Berni, ran Berni's Café in Caerphilly. A previous owner was Joe Bazanni. In the 1930s, the shop served as the Post Office.

106. Lewis Butchers, Trethomas.
Lewis's Butchers shop in Central Buildings, Trethomas, was owned by W.G. Lewis of Bedwas. Mervyn Williams was the manager, seen here with his wife Betty.

107. Worthington's, Bedwas.
Tom Worthington was a locksmith. He opened his first ironmongers shop in Church Street, Bedwas. The assistant in the doorway in this 1927 photograph is Roy Bartle. Notice the range of mining tools which miners had to buy themselves. The shop is now King's Chinese Takeaway.

108. Worthington's, Trethomas.

Tom Worthington gave up his business in Bedwas during the difficult times of the 1930s and started anew in Trethomas. The Trethomas shop stood at the corner of Central Buildings and the Avenue and fine curved windows point to its origin as a men's tailors shop. The current owner is David Morgan. Tom's son Glyn is seen here. This shop supplied hand tools to the British Benzol Plant.

68

109. Williams Ironmongers, Church St.
This shop was on the corner of Tydfil Road, and run by brothers Garnet and Trevor Williams. The figure in the doorway is probably their brother Ithel. The shop stocked general ironmongery as well as scrubbing boards, line props, potty chairs and *Shell* paraffin.

110. Evangeline Williams Church Street.

Dunn's shop, No. 4 Station Terrace, was a general store in upper Church Street, run by Evangeline 'Vengie' Williams (later Dunn). The shop did much tobacco trade with the miners travelling by train to Bedwas Colliery. Notice the tobacco adverts for *Blue Bell*, *Franklins* and *Piccadilly* Cigarettes. 'Twist tobacco off the roll' was a popular buy.

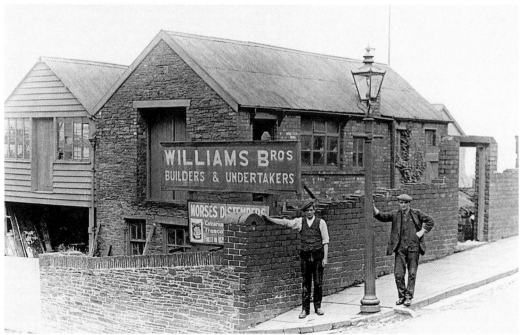

111. Williams Brothers, Undertakers.

Premises of Williams Brothers on the corner of Church Street and Tydfil Road taken about 1939 showing Trevor Williams and Jack Llewellyn. The gable plate shows a date of 1851. The business built many houses in Bedwas and district as well as running an undertakers service, builder's merchants and carpenter's shop. They had the first telephone in the village.

112. Hillside Terrace Shop.

Front room shops were a feature of both villages. This one in Hillside Terrace was run by Mrs. Haines, shown here, and her daughter Vera. It ceased to be a shop in 1939. Quite often, such shops were started with compensation money following a disabling or fatal colliery accident.

113. Bedwas Square, Crown Stores.

Opened as Crown Stores on Bedwas Square, it was divided into two shops for much of its life. In this photograph, the sign shows Tom Hughes' grocery business. The London Joint City and Midland Bank was here for a time, as was Albert Squance, watchmaker and jeweller. Tom Davies' butchery business opened in 1942, later taken over by his son Percy until closure in the 1960s. Crown Dental Surgery now occupies the building.

114. Church Street.
A view north up Church Street in the 1920s. Not a car in sight! The shops include James Emporium (haberdashery and carpets), Worthington's Ironmongery; India & China Tea; Co-operative Stores and Bert Knight Newsagent. The National Provincial Bank stands just beyond the junction with Pandy Road.

115. Morgan's butchers shop.
Tom Morgan is pictured outside his butchers shop at 31 Church Street. The lack of a pavement suggests that it is a pre-World War One photograph. He had farmed at Dyffryn Isaf on the Maesycwmmer Road. He later moved his business across the road to No.20 Church Street in 1920, and then known as 10 Glebeland Cottages. The shop passed to his son, Gwilym Morgan. It was held till recently by David Buckland.

116. Sweet shop, Upper Church Street.

The front of the house at 107 Church Street was extended forward to create a shop, a common practice in the village. In this 1920 photograph, Bella Williams is standing outside her sweet shop.

117. Richards shop and the Library.

Standing at the corner of Church Street and St Mary Street, Will Richards opened an ironmongery and general store in about 1912. He specialised in delivering paraffin oil for lamp lighting, going as far as Rudry, earning him the nickname 'Richards the Oil'. The shop closed in about 1938. The house next door, known to older residents as 'the old library', was the first reading room and library in Bedwas. The words 'Library', 'Institute', 'Powell Duffryn' and 'Llanbradach' (who probably aided the library) can just be made out. It was eventually squeezed out by the much bigger facility at the Workmen's Hall which opened in 1923.

118. Bounds' greengrocers' shop, Church Street.

Bounds greengrocers and general store stood at the corner of Church Street and East Avenue. They also served fish and chips. In the doorway are Alice Davies (nee Bounds) and her children Edith and Horace (on the right). Notice the advertisements for *Fry's Five Boys* chocolate and fireworks. In the 1930s, the shop became Matthew Pavlov's Hay and Corn business, using the large stable on East Avenue for storage. This stable originally held the Council's horse and cart. Later it became Noel and Ewen's garage. Nowadays, it is a doctor's surgery. The shop is now the Bedwas fish and chip shop.

119. Hairdressers' shop, Church Street.

Before he opened the ironmonger's shop, Will Richards had a men's hairdressing and shaving saloon. A pampering shave was especially popular in Edwardian times - perhaps bringing a touch of luxury to otherwise hard working lives. Saturday afternoon at the barbers was a good time for a chat and pipe-smoke and regarded as an entertainment.

120. National Provincial Bank.
This building at the corner of Church Street and Pandy Road replaced some old cottages. Initially called the London and Provincial, it became the National Provincial, and later the National Westminster Bank. It was one of several banks that opened sub-branches in Bedwas and Trethomas with the coming of the colliery. In the foreground is a Mr. Cook.

121. Barclays Bank, Bedwas Square.
Panteg House was the first newsagents shop in Bedwas, later becoming a general store and gents' tailors. Part of the premises became a sub branch of Barclays Bank in 1911 providing a convenient service for the many shops and factories in the village. In common with many other smaller communities, Bedwas no longer has any bank.

122. Barclays Staff.
A June 1914 photograph presented to Mrs. Francis Thomas who kept shop in a room on the left side of the Barclays bank building. Notice the all male staff. In the front row, Mr Phillip Powell the sub branch manager is second from left and the Caerphilly Branch Manager Mr Dyer is second from the right.

123. Van deliveries, 1940.
David 'Dai' Jones delivering greengroceries in Pandy Road near Green Meadow cottage, using an early motorised vehicle with pneumatic tyres and 'stick' wheels. He had a grocers shop next to the Wesleyan (Methodist) Chapel. He earned the nickname 'Dai Taters'. In the days of frequent shopping on foot, a delivery service was much appreciated. His customer is Mary Cook, seen here with her daughter Heulwen.

CHAPTER 5

Education

124. Ty'n-y-wern School, Trethomas, Standard VII, 1916.
This is one of the earliest class photographs of Ty'n-y-wern School. Most of these children, 13 years old, would be 'incomers' - from families recently settled in the new community of Trethomas. Back row (L to R): Jack Essex, ?, Sid Hawkins, ?, Selwyn Rees, Fred Bromage, ?, Jack West, Will Davies. 4th row: ?, Emily Matthews, Annie Sutton, Olwen Rosser, Phyllis James, Edie Knight, Mary Evans, Gwyneth Davies, Cassie Edwards. 3rd row: Mr. Hill, Florrie Gethin, Louisa Palmer, ?, Clara Smart, Gladys Everson, Bessie James, Gwyneth Morris, Winnie Hawkins, Olive Harris, Lena Collins. 2nd row: ?, Billy Gadd, Patsy Dunphy, Ray James, ? Bartlemore, ?, ?, Garfield Williams, ?. Front row: Goronwy Thomas, Sid Burris, Teg Davies, Charlie Ware, Ernie Marshman, George Shaw.

125. Ty'n-y-wern Infants Class IV, 1920s.
A Standard IV class, probably aged 8 to 9 years, with their teacher, Miss Stephens. Large hair ribbon bows were very much in fashion at this time. The girl with the large bow in the back row (4th from right) is Rose Kibby. Front row (L to R); ?, ?, ? Crisp, Tom Crisp, ?, Trewin Shute, ?, ?, ?. One of the Bilton boys is sat in the front.

126. Ty'n-y-Wern Girls school choir, 1924.
The operetta *'The Enchanted Glen'* was probably performed in the spring time after practice through the winter months. The teachers are Margaret Edwards and Graham Beeston. The central higher fairy at the rear is Phyllis Hibbs. Other pupils are: 'Nana' Walters (back row, 2nd left), Bron Powell (next row, 1st left), and Maud Edwards (front row, far left).

127. Ty'n-y-Wern infants class, 1931.
Back row (L to R): Dickie Hodder, Danny Jones, Sidney Phillips, Elwyn Thomas, David Simes, Doreen Baynton, Linda Chisholm, Jessie Hale, ? James. 4th row: Billy Rodgers, Marjory Stallard, Eddie Carter, Billy Perrin, Kate ?, Olga Ryall, May Richards, Audrey Gregory, David Sullivan, Ken Hutchins. 3rd row: Joyce Attwood, Trevor Williams, Fred Coles, Doreen Watts, Dilys Jones, Ken Smith, Joanna Winmill, Melville Bennett, Doreen Goulding, Phyllis Jones. 2nd row: Betty Davies, Margaret Thomas, Gwyn Phelps, Mary Neil, Douglas John, Hazel Brain, Barbara Thomas, Hazel Bowyer, Frank Cooper. Front row: Pearl Hughes, Gladys Shepherd, Morwen Edwards, Odette Rees, Inez Walding, Sadie Rosser, Gwyneth Davies.

128. Standard VII at Ty'n-Wern in 1921.
Back row (L to R): Charlie Ware, Selwyn Rees, ?, Ray James, ?, Pat Dunphy, Sid Hawkins. Middle row: Mr. Hill, ?, Jack Essex, ?, ?, ?, ?, Teg Davies, Sid Burris, Mr. James (headmaster). Front row: Florrie Gethin, Olwen Rosser, ?, ?, Bessie James, ?.

129. A class at Ty'n-y-Wern in 1940.
The adhesive tape crosses on the window panes were to protect those inside from flying glass if bombs fell nearby. Back row (L to R): An evacuee, Frank Cleary, S. Jones, Betty Tucker, Selwyn Bloor, Ira Williams, Olive Rundle, Brian Thomas. 3rd row: an evacuee, June Finch, Vernon Cook, Elwyn Jones, Gertrude Ryall, Des Hodder, Reg Harris, John Morgan, Frances Hutchinson. 2nd row: ?, Trevor Jordan, Elaine Austin, Ray Williams, Cicely Turner, Ray Thomas, Gwen Richards, Pat Cheasty. Front row: ?, ?, Don Watkins, Joan Mormon, Georgina Chisholm, ?, ?, Ann Gardner, John Simmonds. Gwen Richards was one of a family of seven children evacuated from Battersea whose parents also came to live in Trethomas after they were bombed out, and stayed.

130. Girls Domestic Science class at Ty'n-y-Wern, 1938.
Back row (L to R): Connie Nind, Rosie Matthews, ? Waters, Irene Arrowsmith, Joan Wedlock, Babs Bilton, Carol Davies, Joan Fathers, Olga Paul, Mona James. Middle row (L to R): Joan White, ? Vaughan, Pat Pope, Rosie Bird, Joan McGrath, Maureen White, Mary Owen, Mair Price, Alice Palmer, Doreen Baynton, Miss Stephens. Front row (L to R): Marjorie Stallard, Nellie Woods, Marjorie Richards, ?, Elsie Matthews, Glenys Pugh, Rachel Inwood, Clare Blackmore, Beryl Bartholomew.

131. A Ty'n-y-Wern School, 1954.
The building on the right was the domestic science building. Back row (L to R): Betty Rees (teacher), Michael Cheasty, Derek King, Howard Davies, Ken Roden, Gregory Williams, Philip McGuire, Ivor Davies, Ray Davies, David Phillips, Neil Jones, Steven Finch. 2nd row: Noel Hufton, Wendy Jenkins, Lynne Head, Maureen Davies, Celia Jones, Marjory McGuire, Denise Hart, Diane Worthington, Elizabeth Edwards, Cynthia Broughton, Melvyn Inward. 1st row: Annette Richards, Ann Thomas, Marlene Johnson, Katherine Williams, Sian Crispin, June Mead, Doreen Williams, Joan Hunt, Francesca Pole, Glenys Lovell, Angela Humphries, Pat Rowlands. Front row: Royston Powell, Ray Cook, Len Hynam, David Smith, Gary Morris, Michael Hollyfield, Nigel Pritchard.

132. Sports day at Ty'n-y-Wern School in 1967.
School sports day was held on the playing field behind the school. Houses in Lanfabon Drive, the coke works and the benzol plant are visible in the background.

133. Ty'n-y-Wern School
A temporary iron building was erected on this site by the newly-formed Bedwas and Machen UDC in 1913 to provide a school for over one hundred children in families who had arrived in the new settlement of Trethomas. The new school was built in 1915.

134. Bedwas School.
The Alldworth Charity school purchased a lease of a portion of the Bedwas glebe lands to build a new girls school. It had an infants department and another for the older girls who had been taught at Pandy Mawr. The boys had a separate school above the railway on the Mountain Road opened in 1868 and funded by the John Davies Charity. That school closed in 1904 and the boys were accommodated in an extension to the Alldworth Charity's school, the addition on the left side in this picture taken from Pandy Road before any of the new banks and shops were built in 1910 with the sinking of Bedwas Colliery.

135. 'Top School' reunion, Bedwas, 1930.

The John Davies Charity endowed a school for boys built above the church on Mountain Road in 1868. The 'Top School', as it was known, closed in 1903 when the present Junior School was opened in Church Street. For many years after, the 'Top School Old Boys' held an annual reunion supper. In this photograph taken on March 15th 1930, they are assembled in the yard of the Junior School. Present amongst others are Dick Tanner, Charlie Filer, ? Nicholas, Ophne Davies, Dick Nicholas, 'Nen' Filer, W. Cook, John Richards, Wilfred Thomas, Wm. Ashman, John Watkins, Walter Tanner, Thomas Richards, Dick Edmunds, Seth Rowlands, Alf Haines, ? Matthews, Edmund Jones, Tom Jones, ? Cook, Tom Parry, Harry Room, Harry Rees, Will Room, Alf Tanner, Tom Chambers, Charlie Bassett, Jack Jones, Lewis Rose, David Richards, Charlie Smith, Tom Richards, ? Matthews, J. Elder Thomas, Jack Llewellyn, Wm. Jones, Rees Ridout, Will King, Albert King, Edgar Lewis, Gurnos King, Walter Thomas, David Edmunds, Geo Daniels, Ithel Williams, Garnet Williams, Will Richards, Tom Richards, Edmund Edmunds and Ernie Maslen.

136. Pandy Mawr school for girls, 1872.
The first girls' school in Bedwas, endowed by the Allworth Charity, opened in 1809 in the Pandy Mawr Farm House. Miss Rachel Kovachich was appointed school mistress in 1869. Back row (L to R): ?, ?, Miss Rachel Kovachich, Rose Morgan (Ty'n-y-Pwll), Mrs Kovachich, Margaret Davies (Pen-y-Waun). Front row (L to R): a daughter of John 'Sparrow' Jones, ?, ?, ?, ?, Jane Davies (Ty'n-y-Wern), ? Davies (Pandy Rd).

137. Bedwas girls school, about 1900.
A purpose-built school, funded by the Allworth Charity, opened on Church Street, Bedwas, in 1885 and was known as the Bedwas Bridge School. Miss Kovachich was appointed mistress of the girls' department in the new school.

138. Bedwas school, 1903.

Boys have joined the class at the newly enlarged Bedwas Bridge School, complete with starched or laced collars. Four teachers are in this group. This was the era of long exposure photography and some children, unable to sit still, are blurred. The girl almost in the centre of the second row, fifth from the right, is Edith Room (born 1899) who was later to become Headmistress of the Infant School.

139. Teaching staff at Bedwas Bridge School, about 1903.

A staff photograph from just before the retirement of Miss Kovachich in August 1903. At this time, female teachers were required to be unmarried.

140. Bedwas School juniors, about 1920.
Back row (L to R): ?, Cyril Jones, Tom Wakely, ?, Glyn Worthington, Stanley Davies, Fred Cornish, ?, ?, Wm. Maslen. 4th row: Billie Bennett, Dewi Richards, ?, Trevor Williams, ?, Yori Jones, ?, ?, ?, ?, Roy Hughes, Miss Stephens. 3rd row: Kathleen Conville, ?, - Baker, Myrtle Lewis, Maud Evans, ?, Sylvia Cook, ?, ? Bassett (Hillside), Sylvia Phipps. 2nd row: ?, ?, Saranne Jones, - Potter, Barbara Witheridge, ?, ?, Lillian Griffiths, ?. Front row: ?, Len King, Ron Mallett, Nolan Conville, Francis Ashman, George ? (Mary St), ?, Ralph Thomas.

141. The staff of the combined infant and junior schools in 1918.
B. P. Jones joined the school in 1906 and became headmaster in 1914. Miss Ivy Williams was one of several pupil teachers. Back row (L to R): Mr Jones, Miss Phillips, Mrs Jones, Ivy Williams, Harold Lewis. Middle row: Mary Stephens, Gladys Thomas, B. P. Jones, Mably Jones, Evelyn Williams. Front row: Miss Albon, Phyllis Beeston, Edith Room.

142. Bedwas Junior School, about 1953.

Not many class photographs were taken in the immediate post war years. Mr Stephens was headmaster. Back row (L to R): Miss Ivy Williams, Dennis Frost, David Smith, Raymond Palmer, Vernon Sulway, Colin Phipps, Francis Wakely, Gordon Maslen, Graham Frost, Mr Stephens. Middle row (L to R): Malcolm Williams, Jean Evans, Audrey Dobbs, Myra James, Marie Wintle, Gillian Thomas, Margaret Jones, Anne James, Alan Rees, Philip Richards. Front row (L to R): Jean Sweetland, Jacqueline Williams, Barbara Watson, Rosemary Gibbon, Carol Davies, June Mallett, Hilary Golding, Gillian Rutteley, Hilary Hendy, Ann Edmunds, Marie Lewis, Janet Sollis.

143./144. Miss Stephens and the Reception Class, about 1926.

Miss Mary Stephens invariably took the first infants class. At the time of this photograph they were taught in the 'Temporary Building', a large corrugated iron structure in the school yard which lasted many years. Here she has a class of over 50 pupils. The photographer took two photographs from each front corner to include them all. In the top photo the boy in front is an Edmunds. Behind the table are Russ Jones, George Williams, Ken Pritchard, Des Miles, Ernie Millet, and Ken Payne. The girls behind them are ? White, Enid Rosser, ?, ?, and Nancy Griffiths.

CHAPTER 6

Religion

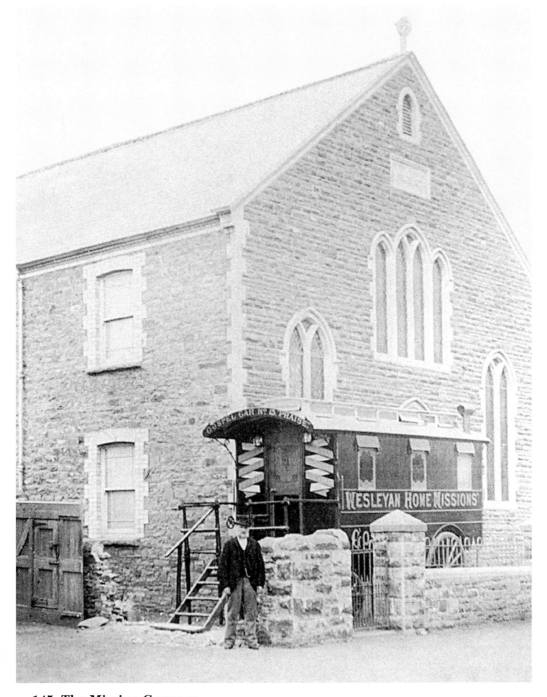

145. The Mission Caravan.
The early Wesleyan Methodists in Bedwas met in the home of Joseph Room at 3 Bakers Row. The first chapel, now the vestry, was built in 1874 and the larger chapel built in front in 1897. It became structurally unsafe and was demolished in 1982, the current church being dedicated in 1987. This photograph shows a visit by the Home Missions Department Caravan, Gospel Car No. 13 'Praise' with an itinerant minister in front, the wall having to be demolished to accommodate it.

146. Interior of The Methodist church, 1960s.

The chapel was known as the Wesleyan Methodist Church until 1932, when a unification scheme changed the title to Methodist Church. Originally part of the Roath Road Circuit in Cardiff, it became part of the Caerphilly Circuit comprising seven chapels in the 1920s. Funds never permitted the building of a gallery as seen in many chapels. The building suffered damage in World War Two when a bomb fell on adjoining land.

147. 'Bright Hour'.

The Wesleyan Church Ladies Fellowship, known as 'Bright Hour', held regular excursions. Hats were still in fashion when this photograph was taken. Back row (L to R): Mrs 'Tom Chas' Davies, ?, Polly Cosslett, Lucy Evans, Mary Ann Phipps, Louie Hale. Front row: Martha David, Lily Mallett, Annie Hale, Martha Jane Maslen.

148. Peniel Chapel.
Peniel Congregational Chapel was built in 1915 in Newport Road, on ground donated by Sir William James Thomas. In common with many chapels of the time, it began as a vestry set back off the road, in anticipation of building a larger chapel in front at a later date. The congregation however did not flourish sufficiently to justify the expenditure. Notice the two columns of protruding stones which would have acted as keys for the main walls. The chapel closed for worship in 1997. It now serves as a day nursery.

149. A Peniel church pageant, 1920s.
On the left stands James Griffiths who conducted the singing at the chapel. Back row: on the left are Gwynfa Evans and Gladys Carter, and from the right Merddyn Evans, ?, Glenys Walter, ?, Charlotte Davies, and Haydn Harries. The tallest girl in the centre of the next row is Allty Williams, and in front of her is Eiry Davies. Front row: Betty Davies and Megan Jones (on the left) and Dwynwen Jones (2nd from right).

150. Primitive Methodist and later Roman Catholic Church.
The Primitive Methodist Chapel, built in 1914, stood in Navigation Street. The church was acquired by the Roman Catholics in 1937 and it was opened as the Church of St Vincent de Paul by the Archbishop of Cardiff. The church closed in 1996 and the congregation transferred to St Helen's Church in Caerphilly.

151. Primitive Methodist Chapel.
This photograph shows the cast of a nativity play. Chapel outings were organised by Walter Starr, whose grocer's lorry could be converted into a charabanc.

152. Whitsun Procession.
On Whitsun Monday, the various churches and their Sunday Schools paraded around the streets, stopping at intervals to listen to preaching and sing hymns. It was an occasion to 'dress up'. The parade was then followed by tea parties and games. The marchers here appear to be singing as they walked. This photograph was taken in 1926, probably in Navigation Street, Trethomas.

153. Salem Welsh Presbyterian Chapel.
Salem Welsh Presbyterian Chapel, founded in 1913, stood at the junction of Standard Street and Navigation Street. It provided Welsh language worship for a considerable number of Welsh speakers who came to work at the Colliery from West and North Wales, many of whom lived in Trethomas. The chapel also provided a focus for Welsh cultural activities.

154. The Forward Movement.

The Forward Movement was an initiative by the Presbyterian Church of Wales to make the denomination more accessible. The building on Standard Street named Trinity, was dedicated in 1916. It was often called 'God Is Love Chapel' because of the words painted on the exterior wall. A small pavilion in the grounds housed the Sunday School. Trethomas Christian Fellowship now worship here.

155. Sister Kate and the ladies of the Forward Movement.

Sister Kate did much to establish the Forward Movement in Trethomas. She exercised an itinerant ministry, staying for about 3 months at a time before moving to another church. Here she can be seen with some of the ladies of the fellowship.

156. Tabernacle Chapel.
The English Baptist Church began meetings in the school's temporary building before they began worship in 1915 in this building at the corner of Newport Road and Bryn-y-Fran Avenue. It was originally the Lucania Billiard Hall. Following its closure, the building was completely demolished in 1997.

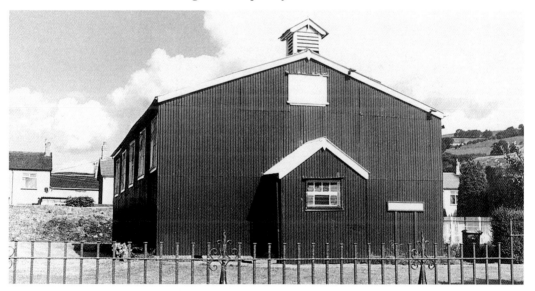

157. The St Thomas Mission Church.
This church opened in 1922 as the Trethomas Mission Church, a daughter church of St Barrwg's. Services were frequently conducted by lay preachers. Corrugated steel churches ('tin churches') were a common feature throughout Wales in the early decades of the twentieth century. Apart from the obvious benefit of being economic to build, some felt that such buildings identified more readily with the new industrial towns and villages. The church was re-titled St Thomas in the late 1980s. It was demolished in 1999 and replaced by a more substantial brick structure which finally opened in 2003.

158. St Barrwg's church.
The parish church of Bedwas was originally a subsidiary of Bassaleg. It was first mentioned in 1102 when it was given to Glastonbury Abbey, and then later to the See of Llandaff. It is dedicated to the seventh century Saint Barrwg, of whom little is known. The church's saddleback tower is a feature found in a cluster of churches in south-east Wales, as well as in Brittany and Normandy. The apex of the tower roof is set transversely to the nave - a very unusual feature.

159. St Barrwg's Choir, 1953.
Back row (L to R): Billy Neighbour (Churchwarden), Harry Brussalis, John Evans, Rector Williams, Colin John, Dennis Bevan, Reg Dean. Middle row: Tyrone Rich, Weldon Davies, Ray Williams, Robert Lewis, Clive Frost. Front row: Graham Frost, Philip Richards.

160. Interior of St Barrwg's church.

The church once had box-type pews with doors, so high that children could only look out by standing on the seats. There were no windows on the north wall and a three-decker pulpit. The clerk, Daniel Lewis, who chewed tobacco, occupied the lowest deck. Prayers were said from the middle position and the sermon preached from the top, when Rector Williams's head was level with the roof. The singing was led by schoolmaster John Rowlands with the aid of a flute, each verse of the hymn being read out first. Rector Williams raised the sum of £1326 to restore the church in 1877. Lord Tredegar and Lord Windsor each contributed £300, and Mr David Morgan of Bedwas Bridge and Rector Williams gave £100 each.

161. St Barrwg's church group and Rector Connop Price, 1920s.

Back row (L to R): Tom 'Trap' Jones, Tom Worthington, G Martin, J Humford, Roy Bartle. Middle row: ? Evans (former PC), ? Bowyer, Frank James (Ty Canol), Rev. Connop Price, Edgar Lewis, Charles Davies-Jones (clerk to the council), Sam Winmill. Front row: Ben Jones, Garnet Williams, ?, ? Hendy (bell ringer), David Jones (Royal Oak).

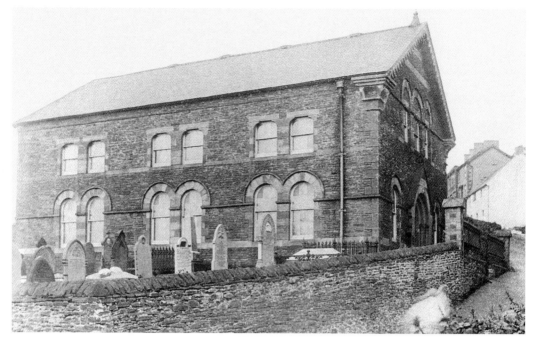

162. Hephzibah.

The Welsh-speaking Baptists of Bedwas worshipped at Hengoed or at Tonyfelin Chapel in Caerphilly until about 1798 when they began holding meetings at Ty Llwyd in upper Church Street. The first Hephzibah Chapel was built nearby in 1844, on a plot of land leased from Dr Joseph Davies of Ty Isaf. Improvements were made in 1857 and again in 1878. A baptistry was added in 1912. Prior to that date, baptisms had taken place in the River Rhymney. Welsh was the predominant language of worship till about 1915. Worship is now conducted in English.

163. Sewing Class at Hephzibah.

Back row, L to R: Mrs Henry Richards, ?, Mrs Willy Richards, ?, Mrs Hill, Mrs Rowlands. Middle row: Margaret Jones, ?, Maggie Hughes (Ty'r Ywen), Mr James (Brooklands), Mrs James, Rev. Jones, ? Simons, ? Richards. Front row: Mrs Beddoe, Vany Jones, Mrs Arthur Richards, ?, Mrs Parry Jones.

164. Bethel Baptist Church.

English-speaking Baptists held the first prayer meetings in the railway station before transferring to the Board School in 1901 for services. The first Bethel Chapel built in 1903, was demolished in 1966 and a new building put up in 1967. The corrugated steel Sunday School building was erected in two stages in 1906 and 1934 at the rear of the chapel. It was replaced by a brick building in 1985.

165. Baptism in the Rhymney River.

Pastor Redman, from Cornwall, was the first minister at Bethel Baptist. Here, he is baptising in the Rhymney River at Bedwas Bridge in 1906. A Baptistry was built at Hephzibah in 1912, probably because of increasing pollution of the river by coal washery waste. Bethel built its own Baptistry in 1944.

166. Saron.
Several Bedwas families of Welsh Independents worshipped at Bethel, Nantgarw Road, Caerphilly. Services then moved to the house of Mr David Gould who took the bardic name of Dewi Aur. Later they met in the Board School until Saron Chapel was built in 1891. Much of the early worship was in Welsh. The bungalow, 'Saronfa', was formerly a cricket pavilion purchased in 1946/47 and erected next to the chapel to serve as a manse. Postman Cliff Barnes is seen on his round.

167. Miles-Ridout wedding at Saron.
Weddings featured in the life of all the churches, such as the marriage of Des Miles and Ann Ridout at Saron in 1947. Back row (L to R): David Edmunds, Tom Miles, Ken Ridout, Garfield Miles, Des Miles, Anne Ridout, Rev. Morris Thomas, Eunice McTeague, Eric Ridout and Greg McTeague, Jack Cornish. Front row: Lizzie Edmunds, Hilda Miles, Mrs Ridout, Nell Cornish.

168. Bethany 1993.
Originally under the Assemblies of God of Great Britain, Bethany Pentecostal Church dates from 1952. The first building was an ex-army hut. Two of the founding members were Bert Reynolds and Emrys Pearce.

169. Full Gospel Mission, Pentecostal Church.
Fellowship of the Assemblies of God of Great Britain at The Crescent, Bedwas. Their early meetings were held in a house in Church Street in the 1920s. Later meetings were held in the Band Room in East Avenue, now a doctor's surgery, and then in an upstairs room in the house next to the garage on Newport Road. A 'tin' church was erected on this site about 1950, and replaced by this building in 1968, here being opened by Mrs Elizabeth Richards. Pictured (L to R) are Bill Jones, Caleb Dando (Chair, A.o.G. South Wales), Janice Williams, Hedley Palmer, Mrs Elizabeth Richards and Colwyn Wilmot (Pastor).

170. Rechabite Group.

Temperance became a major crusade throughout the nineteenth century and well into the twentieth, especially in the Non-Conformist chapels. There was a code of affirmations and often a dress sash. One strategy was to offer a healthy alternative life style. This group was photographed after walking up Mynydd-y-Grug, (Bedwas Mountain). In the top row Ebenezer James is on the far right; Melville Williams, Tom Morgan and Aaron Jones are 3rd and 4th and 7th from the right. In the 2nd row Olive Williams and Lily Williams are 2nd and 4th from the right.

171. Whitsun Monday United Sunday Schools parade.

This was a major village festival for decades, seen here making its way along Celtic Way in the 1950s. A strict rota decided the order of chapels in the procession, especially the one in front. Bedwas United Sunday Schools acquired its own banner in 1937 which is now in the care of the Methodist Church. Clive Maslen carries the right hand pole and Stan Blackwell steadies the guy line of the left hand pole.

CHAPTER 7

Leisure and Entertainment

172. The Bedwas Workmen's Hall Cinema, 1931.
The billboards advertise the *'Prince of Diamonds'*, a romantic drama released in 1930. The cinema had two 35 mm projectors with carbon arc lamp illumination, of which the oldest one has been rescued and is still occasionally used to show films at the Risca Industrial History Museum. Derrick Jones's father came to Bedwas in 1942 from the Rhondda to be the projectionist at the hall. We do not know the identity of this lady in her 1930's fashion.

173. Nantgoch Gleemen at Machen Pit in 1923.
Bedwas Workmen's Hall opened on 3rd December 1923 and included a performance of *'The Flooded Mine'* by the Nant Goch (Trethomas) Male Voice Choir. This photographic pose was taken against the backdrop of the Machen Pit near Green Row, which ironically had closed because of flooding! Left Inset, Edgar Jones (Conductor), Right Inset, W. Milsom (Secretary, Workmen's Hall). Back row (L to R): Bob Jenkins (tenor), Aaron Davies (2nd tenor), ? Lowe, Will Hughes, David Rowland Davies (tenor), Evan Jones (1st bass), Walter Harper of Machen, Abigail Potter (pianist), Esau Davies of Machen, Graham Beeston (bass). Middle row: Tal Bowen (bottom bass), ?, Jim Pugh (bottom bass), Tom Davies (2nd tenor), ?, ?, Dan Gwynne (2nd tenor), ? (boy). Front row: Benny Thomas of Machen (tenor), Billy Weeks, ?, Harold Reid (Secretary & 1st bass), Isaac Thomas (tenor), Bob Davies (1st bass).

174. Bedwas Colliery Glee Party at Bryn Heulog, September 1942.
Bryn Heulog on Mountain Road, Bedwas was rented as the colliery manager's house. This was not long before nationalisation and the manager at that time was Griff Morgan. Back row (L to R): Haydn Davies, H.C. Richards, G.C. Lewis, W.J. Richards, H.G. Ashman, J.S. Blackwell, E.J. Williams, Reg Maslen, E.J.B. Davies. Middle Row: S.M. Thomas, R.W. Clark, W. Chamberlain, P.H. Llewellyn, T.C. Rees, M. Williams, I.C. Jones, J. Richards, Trevor Edmunds, W.H. Jones, F. Blackwell, M.J. Davies, Owen Richards, R.D. Jones. Front row: D.J. Matthews (General Secretary), R.E. Dean (Financial Secretary), Miss G. Edmunds (elocutionist), J. Dawson Griffiths (Conductor), Griffith Morgan J.P. (President), T.W. Jones (Chairman), Dan Richards (Vice Chairman), S.H. Morgan (Treasurer), John Davey (librarian).

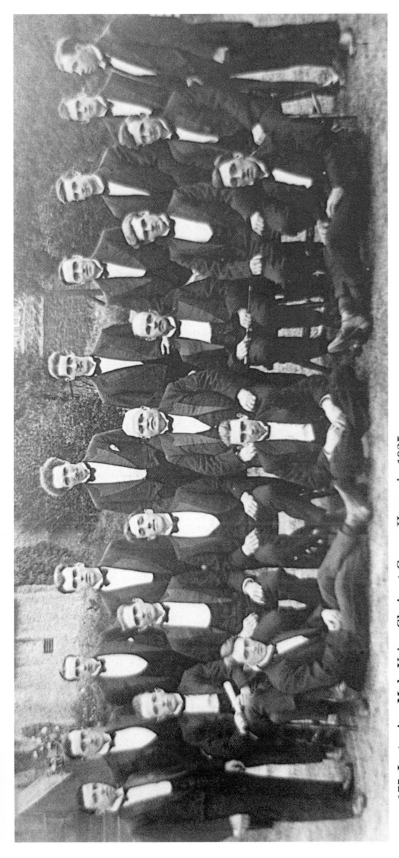

175. Instonian Male Voice Choir at Grove House in 1925.
Sir Samuel Instone became the owner of Bedwas Colliery in 1921. Grove House on Navigation Street, Trethomas, was the house of the Colliery Manager or his Agent. This choir performed under the name of the Instonian Singers. Here, they are posing outside Grove House. The evening dress seems expensive for the time. Was it provided by Sir Samuel? Back row (L to R): Abraham Davies (2nd tenor), Herbert Jones (elocutionist), Uriah Evans (tenor), Trevor Griffiths (tenor), Stan Horton (bottom bass & solo), Jim Pugh (bottom bass & solo), Isaac Thomas (tenor), Evan Jones (1st bass), Aaron Davies (2nd tenor), David Rowland Davies (tenor) . Middle Row: Arthur Jones (pianist), David Rees (1st bass), Bob Davies (1st bass & solo), Harold Lewis (Nelson, President, tenor & solo), Tom Thomas (Conductor), Harold Reid (Secretary & 1st bass), Will Lewis (tenor). Front Row: Tal Bowen (bottom bass), Enoch Jones (tenor), Tom Davies (2nd tenor). David Rowland Davies always stood sideways to be photographed, having lost his right eye in a colliery accident.

176. The lead singers of 'Blodwen' at the Workmen's Hall, 1924.
Several operas were performed at the Workmen's Hall in the 1920s. This photograph
shows the lead singers engaged for the star roles of *'Blodwen'* by Joseph Parry, staged
in 1924. Back row (L to R): T. Timothy, A.B. John (Hon. Sec.), Stan Horton, Isaac
Thomas. Front row: ?, Madame J.T. Harris, Morleisydd Morgan, Madame Bessie
Clee-Williams, David Harry, Madame T. Jones, W. Rees, ?. The conductor was Morris
Llewellyn.

177. 'Quaker Girl' at the Workmen's Hall.
Another opera staged in the 1920s was *'Quaker Girl'*. The full cast of 76 appears on
the steps of the 'Hall' and the conductor was again Morris Llewellyn. The posters
advertised the silent films showing that week at the Workmen's Hall: *'Barbed Wire'*
starring ex-rodeo star Jack Hoxie, the *'Whirlwind Rider'*, released in 1922, *'Men'*
starring the sultry vamp Pola Negri, released in 1924.

178. Bedwas Silver Band outside the 'Royal Oak', 1890s.
Many villages in the 19th century had a silver band and Bedwas was no exception.
Presumably they were based at the Royal Oak. Their uniform was patterned on the
17th Lancers, a regiment often known as the 'Death or Glory Boys', from their part in
the Charge of the Light Brigade during the Crimean War. Godfrey Morgan, later Lord
Tredegar, was one of the survivors of that action. Back row (L to R): Wyndham Rees,
William Ridout, William Burley, Jack Lewis, Joe Mallett, Tudor Thomas, William Rees
(Bandmaster). Front row: Rosser Willie Thomas, Alf Haines, Lewis Jones (Royal Oak),
Alf Hendy, Ted Lewis.

179. The Bedwas and District Silver band, 1944.
This band photographed in the Workmen's Hall field was formed about 1943 and
disbanded in 1951. Back row (L to R): Garnet Ridout, Tom Miles, Arthur Davies, Tom
Adams, Steve Sullivan, Alf Buckley. 3rd row: Bert Fear, Douglas Davies, Les Ashman,
Emlyn Phipps, Trevor Ridout, Bill Mortimer, Ray Davies. 2nd row: Cyril Crane, Len
Bowden, Frank Cottrell, Gerald Jenkins, Rhys Cottrell, Leslie Ridout, Gwilym
Richards, Ken Ridout, John Cornish, Charlie Lovell. Front row (seated): Sam Frost,
Walter Crane, Charlie Francis, Gerald Watts (Conductor), Arthur Richards, Eric
Morgan, George Nightingale.

180. Orchestra.

An orchestra composed of men and women from Machen, Bedwas and Trethomas who performed at the Workmen's Hall. Back row (L to R): George Jones, Reg Minty, Bill Gadd, ?, ?. Middle row: Basil Matthews, Miriam Richards, Graham Davies, Clive Coleman, ?. Front row: Byron Jones, Ivy Denty, Billy Minty, Muriel Williams, Horace Morgan (Secretary), Jim Loftus (Conductor, of Caerphilly), Frank Denty, Dan Burris.

181. A fund-raising 'comic' band at the Workmen's Hall.

The photographer for this pre-WW2 male band was Ivor Curtis, Pandy Road, Bedwas. The 1930s was a turbulent time at the Colliery and the many disputes resulted in long periods of unemployment. Carnivals were a useful way to raise the spirits in difficult times. Band members at each end of the back row bear notice indicating that they were collecting funds either for the International Brigade in the Spanish Civil War or for local hardship relief.

182. Minstrels at the Bedwas and Trethomas Carnival in 1922.
A carnival photo taken on 31st August 1922. This was an all-women affair, with Mrs
Lang, mother of Eileen Hendy, on the far left, Rosie Thomas second from the right
at the rear, and Mrs. Maxwell wearing the trilby. Mrs. (Bert) Jones is believed to be
playing the concertina. The horse and cart belonged to Mr. Thomas.

183. The Bards of the 'Pike', 1939.
A get-together for St David's Day in 1939 in the Club Room on the first floor of the
Ty'n-y-pwll Inn, Trethomas. This is now part of the residential quarters.
Back row: ?, Tom Cooper, Les Davies, Ken Jenkins, Mrs Tanner, Ivor Davies, ? Morgan,
Rose 'the Pike'. Middle row: Parry Williams, ?, Gwilym Morgan, George Beddoe,
Dawson Griffiths, Bob Williams, Emlyn Evans, Arthur Billington, Horace Rogers,
? Coles, ?, ?. Front row: John Evans, Cyril King, ? Thomas, D.J. Davies, ?, Bernard
Stokes.

184. Ambrose Wilson and his Corselettes.
Celebrations for VE Day (Victory in Europe) in May 1945 involved a procession through Trethomas, seen here passing Central Houses, Newport Road. Ambrose Wilson was a manufacturer of a popular corset for the lady with the fuller figure. This good-natured procession reportedly received an objection from the company but it was conveniently ignored.

185. A carnival in the 1950s.
This photograph probably dates from 1951 - the Festival of Britain. The 1950s were the heydays of carnivals as post war prosperity began to lift the gloom of the Depression and World War Two. Here the procession is near the top of Thomas Street. The broom-carrier in front is Archie Hollyfield, whilst the carrier of the tin bath is Abe Roberts (later Councillor). The last carnival was held in 1979.

186. Festival of Britain, 1951.
Back row: Margaret Reynolds, Ann Fitzgerald, Phyllis Harris, Nancy Finch, Doreen Sollis, Marion Sollis, Ann Ryall. Middle row: Norma Matthews, Davina Rich, Trina Harding, Gillian Price, Peter Vaughan. Front row: David Smith, Alun Evans, Mary Palmer, Leonora Williams, Dennis Ryan, Lynette Head, Jacqueline Head.

187. A street party in 1953.
Residents of William Street celebrate the Coronation of Queen Elizabeth II with a street party. At the table are (L to R): Valerie Hayward, Olwen Davies, Myra Davies, ?, ?, Angela Williams. Muriel Williams and Mr. Suttons are behind the table.

188. A street party in 1977.
The street party in William Street, Trethomas, celebrated the Queen's Silver Jubilee in 1977. Minis were still popular but there were not enough cars or traffic to prevent the party going ahead without the need for police permission, which could not happen today.

189. The Carnival Queen's float.
This photograph was taken in Llanfabon Drive en route to Standard Street and Upper Graig-y-Rhacca. Another celebration for the Queen's Silver Jubilee in 1977, all aboard a W. H. Bishop's lorry.

190. Jazz Band Parade, 1970s.
Jazz Bands were especially popular in the 1960s and 1970s. Bands came from many parts of South Wales in good-natured competition. This band, possibly from Coedely, has marched from Addison Way and then along Standard Street. Note the old Sunday School building of the 'God Is Love' Chapel on the left hand side.

191. Billy 'Ferndale' Jones.
Billy 'Ferndale' Jones drove an underground haulage engine at Bedwas pit and enthusiastically trained the local jazz band. He is pictured here conducting the traffic in Trethomas at the junction of Navigation Street and Standard Street on the day of the carnival and jazz bands parade in the 1970s. On one occasion he backed the traffic up all down Navigation Street onto the Newport Road and brought the main road to a complete standstill.

192. Bedwas Townswomen's Guild.
A play about a private school performed on the stage in the Bedwas Pensioners' Hall in the 1950s by ladies of the Townswomen's Guild. (L to R): Sybil Armitage, Maggie Williams, Doreen Wakeley, Margaret Barnes, Bronwen Churchill, Elizabeth 'Bessie' England, Enid Crane, Olwen Rees, Eileen Hendy, Desima Reed.

193. The 'Green Fly' trip to Scotland, 1950s.
Rugby supporters from the Bedwas Workingmen's Club ('Green Fly') en route to the Scotland v Wales international match in Edinburgh in 1951. Back row (L to R): Walter Clist, ?, John ?, Bob Ankers, Cyril Williams, Fred Bartlemore. 3rd row: Tom Grant, ?, Ted Howells, ?, Len Sollis, Ray Sollis, Garfield Moses, Gomer Richards. 2nd row: Des Saunders, Fred Sollis, Bill Brain, Ron Neal, ?, Jacky Morgan, Idwal Fly, Dewi Fly. 1st row: Garfield ?, Dennis Lucy, Tal Hale, 'Kipper' Dunn, Bryn Morgan, ?, ?, Albert Woods. Front: Garfield 'Butch' Williams.

CHAPTER 8

Sporting Activities

194. Bedwas Colliery AFC 1921-22.
Winners of the Trethomas Challenge Cup, the Jack Mills Cup, the Bedwas Challenge
Cup and the Caerphilly League Challenge Cup. Of 35 matches played their record for
the season was 23 won, 5 drawn and 7 lost, with 116 goals scored and 44 against. Back
row (L to R): R. Jones (Asst. trainer), C. Potter (Committeeman), J. Jordan,
B.J. Barnaby, W.J. Milsom, D.A. Harris, R. Bartholomew, W.R. Lewis (Committeeman),
T. Williams (Trainer). Middle row: S. Tanner (Vice-President), E. Cook, G. Witts,
E. Pritchard (Captain), W. Brown, J. Edwards, G.H. McGrath (Hon. Sec.). Front row:
T. Harris, the Bedwas Challenge Cup, D.E. Davies.

195. Trethomas Rangers AFC 1923-1924, First Team.
Back row (L to R): D.E. Davies (Committee), W.J. Lewis (Committee), J. Brown
(Committee), L. Price (Committee), A. Goddard (Committee), J. Ryall, D. Jones,
A. Rosser (Trainer). 3rd row: W. Ryall (Committee), J.M. Davies (Vice-chairman), H.G.
Davies (Chairman), F. Simmonds, G. Passmore (Captain), G. Bond, Giovanni Sartori
(Vice-President), C. Potter (Committee). 2nd row: A. Thomas (Treasurer), T. Catlow,
A. Kendall (Vice-Captain), G. Richards, W. Goodlock, G. Paul, G.E. Davies (Hon. Sec.).
Front row: H. Venn, A. Isaacs, T. Harris.

196. Trethomas Bluebirds Club.
At some stage Trethomas Rangers changed their name to Trethomas Bluebirds. In this 1934/1935 season photograph outside the Workmen's Hall, the Bluebirds had succeeded in reaching third position in the Second Division of the Welsh League, as well as winning the Lady Lewis Cup and the Caerphilly Miners Hospital Cup. Back row (L to R): V Parsons (Trustee), D. Hughes, A. Richards (Committee). 4th row: A.L. Hyman (Committee), E.H. Griffith (Committee), N. James (Committee), J. Sutton (Committee), T.J. Davies (Trustee), F.J. Edwards (Trustee). 3rd row: Gus Smith (Trainer), F. Sutton (Committee), T.H. Baugh, T.J. Sutton, T. Williams, M. Emanuel, I.H. Wall, E.C. Buckley, V. Manuel, D. Cureton, W. Stevens, H. Harding (Treasurer). 2nd row: G.H. McGrath (Secretary), J. Jenkins, D.R. Thomas (Vice-Captain), J.H. Webb (Captain), E. Davies, T.G. Davies, W.H. Lewis (Chairman), J. Hibbert (Vice-President). Front row: C. Cannon, G.A. Clarke.

116

197. British Benzol, 1950s.
The British Benzol Plant in Trethomas ran a useful football team for over two decades. This one dates from the early 1950s. Back row (L to R): Charles Carter, ?, ?, Joe Carter, Mr. Hill, Bill Nind, Maldwyn David, ?, ? Rosser. Front row: Billy Good, Jack Nind, Jack Starr, ?, ?, ?.

198. Trethomas Colts, 1939.
Among supporters and committee in this team photo are four ladies whose help was invaluable, apart from providing the tea and washing the kit. The group on the left are (L to R): Mr. Coles, Mrs. Baynton, Bill Rees, with Warren Hodges in front. Back row (L to R): Rose 'the Pike', Edmund Rowlands, Ron Neal, Henry Coles, Billy Evans, Ron Hyman, Mr. and Mrs. Bartholomew, Miss Sutton, Fred Blackwell, Sally 'the Pike', Mr. Wolfson. Middle row: Harry Harding, Vernon Williams, Charlie Goulding, Vernon Phipps, ? Ryall, Mr. Sutton. Front row: Sam Kedward, Jack Arrowsmith, Gus Arrowsmith.

199. Trethomas Ladies Football, 1933.
Ladies football is nothing new - Trethomas Ladies were pioneering it in the 1930s!
Back row (L to R): Tom Rees, Harry Harding, Mrs. Ethel Hibbs, Phyllis Jones, Mr.
Crudge (ironmonger), Edna Hibbs, Mrs. Dimmock, Mrs. Colwill, Jim Edwards, Edward
Fitzgerald. Middle row: Sid Beynon, Sybil Beynon, Nancy Davies, Phyllis Pope, Phyllis
Hibbs, Mabel Simmonds, Kath Inwood, George McGrath. Front row: 'Poora', Elsie
Matthews, Allty Evans.

200. Trethomas Ladies Football Match.
The Trethomas Ladies in action at an away fixture. Their boots and much of their kit
were borrowed from the Ty'n-y-Wern school team.

201. Trethomas Juniors, 1933-34.
Enthusiasm for football extended to the juniors. The 1933-1934 team carried off the Joshua Morgan Cup as well as the Faccini Cup. Mr Faccini was the Italian proprietor of the café in Trethomas. Back row (L to R): Jack Nind, Ron Hyman, Len Sully, Vernon Phipps, Reg Matthews, Byron Williams. Front row: Sam Kedwards, Stan Nind, Eddie Jenkins, Archie Hollyfield, Teddy Smith.

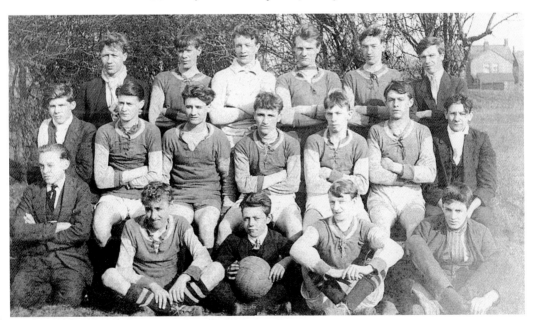

202. Bedwas Junior Team, Chas Richards Capt.
One of the Bedwas Soccer teams playing on the Oak Field in Bedwas around 1918. Part of the dividing field hedge had been removed to make a full size playing pitch. Part of it still remains as a photographic backdrop. Back row (L to R): Ivor French, Trevor Morris, Gwyn Passmore, Reg Maslen, Arthur Williams, Glyn Mallett. Middle row: Will Maslen, Eli Tanner, Trevor Evans, Charles Richards, Jack Colley, George Bond, Eddie Nicholas. Front row: Stan Morley, Levi Barnet, Stan Thomas, Jack Davies, Norman Martin.

203. Trethomas Baseball Team.
Baseball gained in popularity during the 1930s and both Trethomas and Machen had teams. This photograph was probably taken in front of the Colliery wall. Back row (L to R): Cyril Jones, Bryn Griffith, Colston Buckley, Clem Powell, Pat Partridge, Alf Cook, Jack Ryall. Front row: Arthur Dimmock, Barney Jones, Percy Hyman, Elwyn John, John Jones.

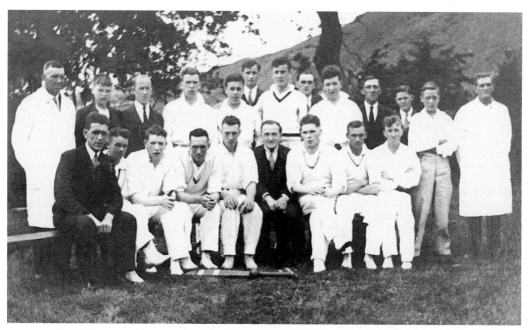

204. Trethomas Cricket Club 1935.
The cricket pitch was sited north west of the football field where Bryn-y-Fran Avenue and Llanfabon Drive now stand. An old railway wagon at the Ash Grove end served as a changing room. Back row on left, J. Matthews, umpire. Front row (L to R): D. Richards (Chairman), G. 'Butch' Williams (Captain), Harry 'Fochriw' Jenkins, T. Allsop, E. Fitzgerald (President), Mr Wolfson (President), W. Colwill, G. Price, H. Matthews.

205. Bedwas Colliery AFC Officials, 1921.
This photograph of a colliery officials' team has the suggestion of a 'scratch side' with striped jerseys possibly borrowed from a local rugby team. BNC chalked on the football stands for Bedwas Navigation Colliery. Far left in the back row is 'Spark' Tanner, an electrician at the colliery and landlord of the Ty'n-y-Pwll Inn.

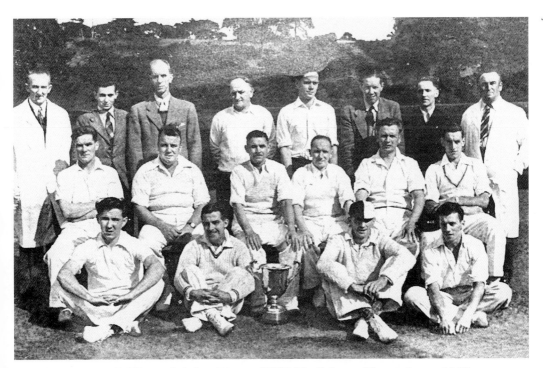

206. Bedwas Colliery Cricket Team, NCB No.5 Area Champions, 1948.
Back row (L to R): ?, Colwyn Wilmott, Reg Dean, Dai Walters, Tony Jones, Reg Davies, Gwilym Pritchard, Cyril Gregory. Middle row: Wyndham Colwill, Monty Matthews, Reg Jones, Tom Isaacs, Les Vaughan, Phillip Francis. Front row: John Williams, Dewi Jones, Stan Blackwell, Glyn Davies.

207. Bedwas Cricket Club.
Cricket was first played in Bedwas on the Trapwell Field until the 1930s. Other teams played on the Oak Field, off Pandy Road, then known as the Royal Oak Ground. This photograph is thought to have been taken in the early 1930s. Courtney Williams is the schoolboy sat in the front on the left and his father Trevor is seated on the right. Edgar Lewis of Troedyrhiw House, the club president, is fourth from the right in the middle row. At the rear are Dai 'Aberdare' Jones (wearing a trilby) and Billy Milsom (wearing a cap).

FIXTURES.				Scores			SEASON'S RECORD.
Date, 1919.	Opponents.		Gr'nd.	For.	Agst.	Ind.	
May 3	Trial Match	..	home				
10							Won ....
17	Dinas Powis	..	away				
24	Penhill C.C., Cardiff	..	home				
31	Spillers C.C., Cardiff	..	home				Lost ....
June 7	Ryder C.C., Cardiff ..	..	away				
W.M. 9	Bream (Glos.)	..	home				Drawn ....
14	Ystrad Mynach	..	home				
21	Cardiff Victoria	..	home				
28	Fleur-de-lis	..	home				
July 5	Ystrad Mynach	..	away				
12	Cardiff High School Old Boys	..	home				
19	Penhill C.C., Cardiff	..	away				Total ....
26	Dinas Powis	..	home				
Aug. 2	Fleur-de-lis	..	away				
9	Bream (Glos.) Annual Outing	..	away				Runs for ....
16	Cardiff Cliftonians	..	home				
23	Ryder C.C., Cardiff	..	home				
30	Cardiff Victoria	..	home				Runs against ....

MEMBER'S CARD.

L. S. Jones Esq.
Vice-President

208. Bedwas Cricket Club programme, 1919.

209. Bedwas RFC, about 1900.
Most of the jerseys were harlequin pattern and jodhpur-style shorts were the order of the day. Hob nailed working boots are the most common footwear. Leather bars, home made, can be seen third from the left front row. Seated on the right is David Edmunds of Sebastopol Cottage. The man with the bowler hat is probably David Jones of the 'Royal Oak'.

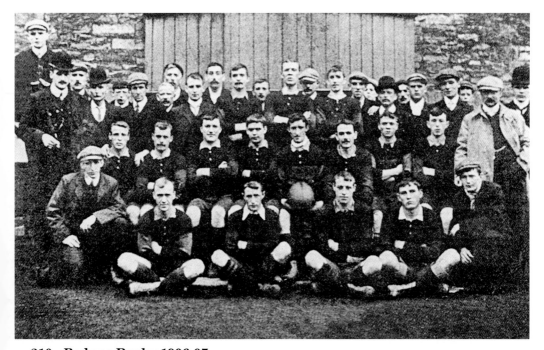

210. Bedwas Rugby 1906-07.
Bedwas Rugby Club was officially recognised by the Welsh Rugby Union in 1889. This is one of the earliest photographs of the club, a medal-winning side dating from 1906-07 season. Garnet Williams is second from left in the middle row.

211. Cartoon by J.C. Walker from the South Wales Echo, December 24th 1932.

212. Bedwas Rugby Club, 1921-1922.
This photograph shows the 1921-1922 side outside the Bridgend Inn when Harry Lewis was landlord. Front row (L to R): ?, Charlie England, Billy 'Dowlais' Lewis, Albert King, Tom Miles. First row (seated): Albert Bushen, ?, ?, George Filer, ?, Bill Cosslett, ?, Bill Crane, ?. The trainer is Alf Miles, with Charlie Richards on his right. 'Nen' Filer is on the right in the doorway.

213. Bedwas Rugby, April 1925.
Billy 'Dowlais' Lewis was the trainer when this team photograph was taken in the yard of the Bridgend Inn. They changed in a corrugated iron shed behind the inn. In the back row is Lyn Thomas (4th right). In the front row are George Hendy and Reg Maslen (2nd & 3rd left).

214. Bedwas Ex-Schoolboys RFC.
An Ex-Schoolboys Rugby side of about 1920 at Rodney Parade, Newport. The players are:- Back row (L to R): D. Williams, T. Brown, G. Nicholas, T. Evans, M. Brown, E. Marsh, ?. 2nd row: Cyril Williams, G. Hendy, S. Thomas, Horace Williams, Lyn Thomas, C. Filer, H. Crane. Front row: 'Ted' Williams, ?, N. Williams. The committee men are A. Llewellyn, M. Bennett, F. Walden, W. Rich, W. Williams, A. Churchill, M. Bushen, G. Davies, T. Davies, S. Thomas and T. Cosslett.

215. Bedwas Rugby Club, 1947.
Bedwas Rugby played for a few seasons after World War Two on the Rectory Field, now Bryn Glas and Bryn Fedw, before finally moving to their present home at the Bridge Field on Newport Road. This photograph is reputedly in honour of a new set of jerseys! Back row (L to R): Sid Hale, Ron Curnow, Arthur Minty, Viv Thomas, Referee, Ticker Ryall, Ralph Sharples, Ivor Lumber, Arthur Martin. Middle row: Tommy Ashman, Garfield Cosslett, Tommy Isaac, Bill Willets, Ralph Mallett, Jack Price, Ron Willets. Front row: Tommy Whitefoot, Percy Heath, Tom Roberts, Hywel Lewis.

216. Bedwas RFC, mid 1960s.
The team pose for a photograph outside the new brick-built clubroom which replaced the ex-RAF hut obtained from St Athans in the early 1950s. Back row (L to R): Derek Harper, Bill Davies, Keith Edwards, Alan Kenyon, Glyn 'Bonzo' Jones, Ronnie Dunn, Brian Howells, Dennis Pritchard. Middle row: Michael Brock, David Thomas, Colin Stenner, Edwin 'Eddie' Lewis, John Dunn, John Hughes. Front row: Bobby Boyland, John 'Jack' Matthews.

217. Bedwas Miniature Rifle Club.
This photograph was taken about 1912 behind the Bridgend Inn with 'Corker's Cottage' in the background. Will Mallett is wearing his medals gained at the Battle of Belmont during the Boer War. Back row (L to R): A. Haines, D. Jones, D. Simes, W. Palmer, W. Burley. Third row: G. Ridout, T. Carder, T.C. Davies (Referee), I. Thomas (Secretary), A. Churchill (Captain), Z. Thomas (Chairman), E.J. Lewis (Treasurer), W. Mallett (Superintendent), G. Williams. Second row: Vice-Presidents - H.G. Thomas, A.W. Lewis, W.G. Lewis, Dr. J.S. Nolan, J. Morgan. Front row: J. Williams, S. Harris, T. Richards, T. Taylor, J. Hardacre, A. Strange.

Acknowledgements

Some of the photographs are from the authors' collections but many are the treasured family photographs of residents in Bedwas and Trethomas which have been borrowed and copied over the last 30 to 35 years. It would be fair to say that we do not know the present whereabouts of many of these photographs and that some may have been lost over the years. We have chosen not to name the people who loaned us their photographs or given generously their time and knowledge in case we unintentionally forget someone and thereby cause offence, but thank you one and all.

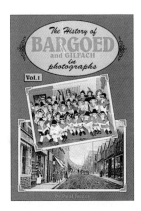
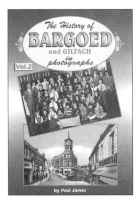
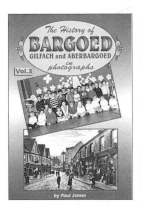

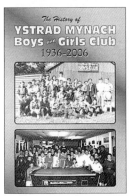
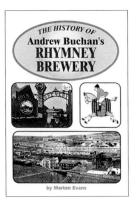

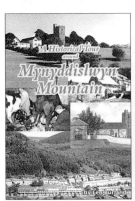

A small selection of many other titles available from Old Bakehouse Publications.